Cults & Other Beliefs

by Bruce Frederickson

Contents

Session 1   What Do I Believe?   3
Session 2   Established Cults   6
Session 3   Modern Christian, Eastern, and Science Cults   9
Session 4   Satanic Cults   13

Cover art by Karen Pauls

Prepared by the staff of the Board for Parish Services, The Lutheran Church—Missouri Synod

Written by Bruce Frederickson
Edited by Thomas J. Doyle
Editorial assistant: Phoebe Wellman

Write to Library for the Blind, 1333 S. Kirkwood Road, St. Louis, MO 63122-7295 to obtain *Cults and Other Beliefs* (Student Book) in braille or in large print for the visually impaired.

Scripture quotations in this publication are from The Holy Bible: NEW INTERNATIONAL VERSION, copyright © 1973, 1979, 1984 by the International Bible Society. Used by permission of Zondervan Bible Publishers.

Copyright © 1990 Concordia Publishing House
3558 S. Jefferson Avenue, St. Louis, MO 63118-3968
Manufactured in the United States of America

All rights reserved. No part of this publication may be reproduced, stored in a retrieval system, or transmitted, in any form or by any means, electronic, mechanical, photocopying, recording, or otherwise, without the prior written permission of Concordia Publishing House.

1   2   3   4   5   6   7   8   9   10   **CPC**   99   98   97   96   95   94   93   92   91   90

What Do I Believe?

DISCOVERY POINT

God reveals Himself to us in His Word. By the power of the Holy Spirit working through the Word, God creates and sustains saving faith in Jesus Christ, thereby providing forgiveness of sins and eternal life.

TRUE OR *FALSE*

Did you know that each of the statements made by the people shown above is false? Try making each of the statements true. If you can't make a statement true at this time, try again at the end of this session.

WHAT IS FAITH?

1. In your own words, describe "faith."
2. What is the difference between "faith" and "religion"?
3. Read **Heb. 11:1**. How does the writer of Hebrews define faith?

How does the writer describe faith in **Heb. 11:1–40**?

Do you ever demonstrate faith similar to God's Old Testament people? How?

4. Once a Roman military officer approached Jesus, begging Him to heal his servant. Read **Matt. 8:5–13** to find out how the officer demonstrated his faith.

How did the officer respond to Jesus' offer to visit the sick servant **(vv. 8–9)**?

THE OBJECT OF FAITH

The following letter was found in a baking powder can wired to the handle of an old pump which offered the only trace of drinking water along a seldom-used trail across the Amagosa Desert.

To Whom It May Concern:

On this day, June 3, 1932, the pump works. I put a new sucker/washer into it that ought to last five years or so. But the washer dries out and the pump needs to be primed. I buried a bottle of water under the white rock, out of the sun, with the cork end up. There's enough water in it to prime the pump, but not if you drink some first. Pour about one-fourth of the water onto the washer and let it soak into the leather. Then quickly pour on the rest and pump like crazy. You'll get water. The well has never run dry. Have faith! When you have had enough water, fill the bottle and put it back like you found it for the next person.

[Signed,]
Desert Pete

P.S. Don't drink the water in the bottle. Prime the pump with it, and you'll have all the water you could ever want.

1. If you had arrived hot and tired at this pump, what would you have done? Would you have been tempted to disregard the instructions and drink the water in the bottle? You've walked for miles with no water. Your mouth is parched and dry. And who is this "Desert Pete" anyway? Can you have faith in what he says?

2. How does this story describe faith? Is faith something you can see, touch, taste, or smell? If not, how can you ever know exactly what faith is? Read **Rom. 10:14–17** to help you answer these questions.

If you thought the questions above were easy to answer try the following

Bonus question: Like a pump, how is your faith primed?

Notice that faith must have an object. Faith is always "in" something, such as people, objects, ideas, and God.

3. What does it mean to believe in God? Does faith in God include more than a belief that God exists? Does the devil believe in God? Read **James 2:19**. Although the devil believes that God exists, his "faith" results only in fear. What does Luther mean by the word *fear* in the beginning of his explanation to the Ten Commandments included in the Catechism? How is the fear Luther tells us we should have different from the devil's fear of God?

4. Read **1 John 5:13**. What certainty does God want our faith to include? Some people have strong faith that God will take them to heaven when they die but are troubled with many problems in "this life." They struggle with doubts about themselves, their future, and their relationships with others. When does eternal life, promised by Jesus in **John 3:16,** begin? Is it something far off or right here and now, or both?

5. Your best friend tells you that he/she is having trouble believing that Jesus really cares about him/her, because of all the trouble he/she has been having. What assurance can you give your friend?

PUT YOUR MONEY WHERE YOUR MOUTH IS!

What does the saying, "put your money where your mouth is," mean? Have you ever loaned money to a friend and then lost hope that you would ever get the money back? Would you trust your "absent-minded" friend with more money after he or she has repeatedly "forgotten" to pay you back?

Put your money where your mouth is! If you "say" you trust your friend, then "prove" it! If you "say" you believe in God, then "prove" it! What is the proof of your faith in Christ Jesus **(James 2:14–26)?**

Read and discuss the following story about the great tightrope walker, Blondin:

Sometime during the last century the great tightrope walker, Blondin, agreed to walk across Niagara Falls on a tightrope without the aid of a safety net. With cheering crowds lining both the Canadian and United States sides of the falls, Blondin carefully made his way out over the windy chasm, then cautiously walked back. To the wild approval of the fans, Blondin announced that he would again "walk over the falls" with the additional weight of a chair strapped to his back. A hush fell over the crowd as he began his second trip. Again, to the amazement of almost everyone present, he successfully completed a second round trip to the wild cheering of the onlookers. He stepped to the front of the crowd and said that he would make one more trip with a person seated in the chair still tied to his back. The crowd shouted its approval and confidence *until* he asked, "Who will volunteer to ride in the chair?"

1. If you had been in the crowd that day, would you have volunteered? Why or why not?

2. How does this story describe faith in Jesus? Does this story describe **your** faith in Jesus? Describe a time when you were willing to cheer for Jesus, but unwilling to get on His back and allow Him to carry you over your problems. Luther stated in a sermon based on **Gal. 4:1–5,**

Faith is the yes of the heart, a conviction on which one stakes one's own life . . . But this faith does not grow by our own powers. On the contrary, the Holy Spirit is present and writes it in the heart.

We can talk about religion and cheer from the sidelines. But it is only through faith that we are able to depend completely on Jesus to carry us across the many chasms we must face in this life. These

chasms include temptations, frustrations, fears, and disappointments. The Holy Spirit works through God's Word to strengthen faith. If you are troubled, turn to God's source of strength, the Bible, and receive the faith-strengthening power of the Holy Spirit.

DO YOU KNOW WHAT YOU BELIEVE?

1. The American Bankers Association offers a special 10-day class to teach bank tellers how to identify counterfeit money. Interestingly enough, for the first nine days of the class, no one is shown counterfeit money. Everything they handle and examine is real. Only on the last day of the class is counterfeit money mixed with the real money. Why is the counterfeit money only shown to the students on the last day?

This is a four-session course on cults and other religious beliefs. Why is it important to discuss what *you believe* before studying what others believe?

2. Do you know what you believe? Suppose you encounter an automobile accident. While help is summoned, you are left alone with the severely injured victim. He expresses doubt about God, faith, and eternal life. He fears death. What would you tell this person? Think about it. In a short paragraph write what you could say to comfort the victim as you witness your faith in Christ Jesus.

TO REVIEW AND REMEMBER

The First, Second, and Third Articles of the Apostles' Creed with explanation.

FAMILY TIME

1. Look up the word *cult* in the dictionary. Ask family members to define and give examples of cults. Were there cults when your parents were growing up? Why have cults become so popular today? Read together **2 Tim. 4:1–4** as you ponder these questions.

2. If someone very special were to write a letter to your family, would you take time to read it? Someone very special has written some words especially for you and your family. During the coming week, spend time reading God's Word together as a family. Some suggested readings are as follows:

- [ ] Day 1: **Gen. 3:1–15.** Our sin/God's promise.
- [ ] Day 2: **Eph. 2:1–10.** We are saved by grace.
- [ ] Day 3: **1 Cor. 12:1–11.** Through faith we confess Jesus Christ.
- [ ] Day 4: **James 1:19–27.** What is true religion?
- [ ] Day 5: **Matt. 14:22–36.** Don't be afraid!
- [ ] Day 6: **Prov. 14:10–18.** What seems right isn't always correct.
- [ ] Day 7: **John 14:1–7.** Jesus is the only way!

Established Cults

DISCOVERY POINT

God clearly reveals Himself in His Word, offering His promise of forgiveness of sins and eternal life through faith in Christ Jesus.

ITCHING EARS

Have you ever suffered from a disease or allergy that caused you to itch uncontrollably? Two of the frames have young people suffering from severe itching. How is the third frame related to the first and second? Read **2 Tim. 4:3–4**. St. Paul describes people who listen to false teachers as people who hear "what their itching ears want to hear." How is the itching of people's ears described in **2 Timothy** similar to the itching caused by a rash or a disease?

Each of the following is an "itching ear" word that describes either a group of people suffering with itching ears or a symptom of people suffering from itching ears. Test your ability to match correctly each of the "itching ear" words with its definition or description. Check your answers after completing this session.

_____ 1. cult

_____ 2. heresy

_____ 3. Mormons

_____ 4. Pelagians

_____ 5. Arians

_____ 6. Jehovah's Witness

_____ 7. Christian Scientist

a. an opinion or teaching contrary to the church's teaching
b. followers of the teaching of Joseph Smith
c. "splinter group" from the Christian church
d. believes in teachings contained in Mary Baker Eddy's book, *Science and Health with Key to the Scriptures*
e. followers of an ancient heresy condemned at the council in Nicea in A.D. 325
f. believed Jesus was true God, but not true man
g. religion whose members meet in Kingdom Halls and distribute literature door-to-door across the United States and the world.

CULTS BEGIN

What is a cult? Do you know someone who is a member of a cult? How do cults form?

1. Cults have been around for a long time. Soon after Christ founded His church and returned to His Father, "cults"—or splinter groups—began to form. Before His ascension, Jesus settled the disputes of His disciples personally. Once Jesus ascended, His disciples relied on His Word to settle disagreements.

Divisions began to occur. By the beginning of the fourth century, a church leader named Arius taught that Jesus was not divine (God), but only a very special human being chosen by God. Arius believed that Jesus was no different than other devout human beings. In A.D. 325, at a church council (meeting) in Nicea, the teachings of Arius were condemned. The Nicene Creed was adopted as a complete statement to defend the teachings of the Christian church and to reject the teachings of Arius.

What is the longest section (article) of the Nicene Creed? Why did the council feel it was necessary to go into such great detail about the person and work of Jesus Christ? Notice that the Nicene Creed contains some very specific terminology about both Jesus' humanity (true man) and deity (true God).

2. Other cults quickly followed the Arian controversy. The Pelagians believed that Jesus was true God, but rejected His humanity. They spread their teaching into many parts of the church. Their false and unbiblical teachings spread rapidly before church councils and inquisitions could stamp them out.

3. The anti-Trinitarians denied the Trinity—the "three-in-oneness" of God. They argued that since the Bible did not use the word *trinity*, God could not possibly be triune. The orthodox Christian church, those faithful to the Word of God, responded with the Athanasian Creed. What teaching of the church does the Athanasian Creed emphasize?

4. Since its beginning the Christian church has firmly responded to false teachings (heresies). Individual Christians and groups of Christians (councils) have responded to heresy with clear and useful documents called confessions.

Satan remains persistent. In his attempt to tear down and render Christ's work on earth ineffective, the devil perpetuates more lies. For how long has our enemy, the devil, worked overtime trying to cause people to doubt, destroying the faith which God creates **(Gen. 3:1–4, John 8:44)**? It is no wonder that cults have broken away from the fundamental teachings of Christ's church.

JEHOVAH'S WITNESSES

1. In 1879, when Charles Taze Russell began publishing a magazine called *Zion's Watchtower*, he had been leading a small Bible study group for some time. Russell and his little group struggled with some Bible teachings (doctrines) and finally reached several conclusions which were opposite those of orthodox Christianity.

Russell taught that Jesus was only human, and therefore could not forgive sins, heal sick people, and rise from the dead. Russell said that the Trinity was an idolatrous work of the devil and really the worship of three separate gods. Russell's little group, later known as Jehovah's Witnesses, denied the existence of hell as a place of suffering. Which of the ancient heresies condemned earlier by the Christian church does the doctrine of the Jehovah's Witness resemble?

2. Leadership of the Jehovah's Witnesses passed from one bold leader to another after the death of Charles Taze Russell. Further refinements of their teachings continued to emerge. Many books and magazines were added to their collections under the leadership of Joseph Franklin Rutherford. Most recently, under the guidance of Nathan Knorr, this once little group has grown to over two million.

3. Jehovah's Witnesses are well known for their meeting places, called Kingdom Halls, and their zeal for distributing literature door-to-door across the United States and the world. None of their workers receives a salary. All members are called "ministers" and "publishers" because all are expected to serve and distribute literature.

4. You don't talk to a Jehovah's Witness very long before you realize he/she knows Scripture well. Yet Jehovah's Wittnesses do not understand the central message of the Bible. They freely quote Scripture without considering the context.

(What does it mean to take the meaning of something out of context? Has anyone ever repeated something you said out of context, giving people the wrong impression about what you meant by your statement?)

5. Jehovah's Witnesses deny one of the most basic and important Christian teachings, Christ's physical resurrection from the dead. Instead, they suggest that Christ only rose "spiritually" from the dead. If a group rejects the deity of Christ, what central teachings of the church are destroyed?

6. When Jehovah's Witnesses, visit your home, they are looking for several things. They want money in exchange for their literature. They want time in discussion at the door, and they will offer to conduct a Bible study in your home. They want you to agree with them about the strange teachings they present.

7. Read **Eph. 1:22, 2:4–7, 2:20, 4:15; Col. 1:18;** and **Phil. 2:5–11.** What teachings of the Christian church do these passages defend

against the heresies of the Jehovah's Witnesses cult?

MORMONS

1. The Mormon Church is well known in America. Otherwise known as the Church of Jesus Christ of Latter Day Saints, it was begun by a young man named Joseph Smith. Smith was troubled by the conflicts between various denominations and confused about which church to join.

According to Mormon history, the angel Moroni visited Smith while he was deep in prayer. Moroni told Smith that all religions were wrong, and God chose him to reveal the true religion to the world. Years later, following several subsequent visions, Jesus appeared to Smith and directed him to find and dig up a package of special gold plates written in an ancient Egyptian language. Although Smith could not read the plates, the package also contained a pair of spectacles enabling Smith to read and translate the writing. He later published it as *The Book of Mormon.*

2. Religious persecution against the small cult that Smith founded forced them to migrate from New York to Ohio, and later to Illinois. When Smith was killed, the group split into two groups. One group followed Smith's son, Joseph Smith, Jr., to Kansas City, Missouri, forming the Reorganized Church of Jesus Christ of Latter Day Saints. The larger of the groups remained faithful to Smith's teachings and followed Brigham Young to Utah. Today the Mormon Church has a vast agricultural, financial, and genealogical empire.

3. Mormons may call themselves Christian, but their teachings are definitely not Christian. Mormons believe that Jesus was only a person. They consider the Trinity a pagan attempt to explain the unexplainable. How do the teachings of the Mormons resemble those of Jehovah's Witnesses? What ancient heresy(ies) does Mormonism resemble?

While accepting the Holy Bible, Mormons believe the Bible can only be understood in light of the *Book of Mormon.* Mormons, therefore, place Joseph Smith's words above God's Word in authority.

4. Mormons talk about Christ's death for them, but they also teach "works-righteousness," the need to perform sufficient good works in order to merit entrance into heaven. Since the Mormon heaven has many levels, ambitious members can receive greater reward if they perform more good works. No member can ever be assured that he or she has done enough to merit forgiveness of sins and eternal life. Read **Eph. 2:8–9** and compare the Biblical teaching of forgiveness and eternal life with the Mormon teaching. Which teaching provides confidence and comfort to the troubled sinner?

CHRISTIAN SCIENCE

1. Preoccupied with sickness and death after her husband died, Mary Baker Eddy founded a cult in 1876 called Christian Science.

Certain that she too was soon going to die, Mrs. Eddy fell under the influence of a healer/doctor named Phineas P. Quimby who healed her by treating her diseased body parts with magnets and positive psychological suggestion.

When Quimby died, Eddy claimed to have discovered how to heal people. She published a book called *Science and Health with Key to the Scriptures*, which claimed that Jesus used the same principles in healing. The cult grew rapidly as middle-aged and elderly people sought healing from their diseases. Eddy began her own college, the Massachusetts Metaphysical College, to promote and spread her heretical teaching of divine healing.

2. While Eddy claimed that the Bible was her only teacher, she said that God, who authored the Bible, is not a being at all. She described God as a series of thoughts and feelings making up matter and energy. Since God is good, reasoned Eddy, He created everything and everyone good. Evil doesn't really exist. Sickness exists because people have a wrong idea of God, and death is not real. How does the teaching of Mary Baker Eddy eliminate the need for a Savior?

TO REVIEW AND REMEMBER

Continue review of the three articles of the Apostles' Creed and their explanation.

FAMILY TIME

God provides a way for your faith and the faith of your family to remain strong. Read together the suggested portion of the Bible each day. Pray for the Holy Spirit to keep you faithful in His Word, protect you from involvement in cults, and enable you to witness your faith to those who are members of cults.

- Day 1: **John 10:1–6.** The sheep know their Shepherd.
- Day 2: **John 10:7–18.** Jesus is the Good Shepherd.
- Day 3: **Rom. 1:18–28.** Worship the Creator.
- Day 4: **2 Tim. 3:10–17.** Continue in what you have learned from God's Word.
- Day 5: **Acts 20:27–31.** Wolves will seek to devour Christ's flock.
- Day 6: **Matt. 24:45–51.** The Holy Spirit keeps you faithful until Jesus returns.
- Day 7: **Rom. 12:1–8.** God desires you to be His own.

Modern Christian, Eastern and Science Cults

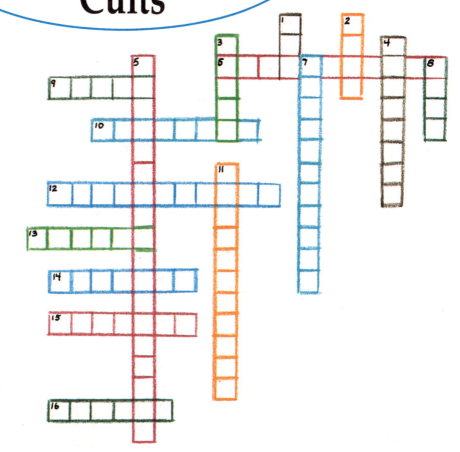

DISCOVERY POINT

God promises forgiveness of sins and abundant life now and in eternity through faith in Jesus.

REVIEWING THE ORIGIN OF CULTS

The crossword puzzle will help you review the origin of modern cults, which are 50 to 150 years old, and will introduce terms which you may wish to use when witnessing your faith in Jesus Christ.

INTRODUCTION TO "NEW" CULTS

Many "new" cults began during the "Jesus people" movement of the 1960s. This movement began as a positive force by young people who were discouraged by the lifelessness and inactivity of the organized church. Members of the movement, often called "Jesus freaks," encouraged public confession of faith and distributed leaflets on street corners, in coffee houses, in bus depots, and on college campuses. They were eager to help everyone "know Jesus."

As the "Jesus people" movement gained momentum, some individuals seized the opportunity to achieve profit and influence at the expense of others who were innocent and committed to witnessing their faith in Jesus. Strong leaders emerged within these growing groups whose motive was often personal gain. Literally

Across

6. Received only by God's grace through faith in Jesus Christ.
9. Visited by the angel Moroni.
10. Ancient heresy condemned at the Council of Nicea in A.D. 325.
12. Received only through the suffering and death of Jesus on the cross.
13. The cult established by Joseph Smith.
14. Condemned the teaching of Arius.
15. Leader of the Jehovah's Witnesses.
16. An opinion or teaching contrary to scripture.

Down

1. Itching _____ .
2. "Splinter" group from mainline Christian churches.
3. Redeemer.
4. The only reliable source of information concerning the person and work of Jesus Christ.
5. Founded by Mary Baker Eddy.
7. Written and adopted to defend the teachings of the Christian church against Arianism.
8. Wrote *Science and Health with Key to the Scriptures*.
11. Believed Jesus was true God but not true man.

hundreds of cults began during this time, splintering from Christianity and other major religions.

Among the groups which splintered from the Christian church were The Children of God (Family of Love), The Unification Church (Moonies), and The Way International. The Hare Krishna cult splintered from Hinduism and Zen. Many more cults began without a formal name or title.

During the 1960s it became clear that people were looking for something that the Christian church did not seem to provide. Some cults attracted many people because of the free and easy lifestyle they offered. The leaders of these groups often preyed upon the dependency of the individuals that followed them. Once committed, most cult followers willingly did anything for their leader, including violating their own consciences.

Many of the recruits to cults were kids who were having problems in school, at work, and at home. They didn't like the authority of parents, teachers, and police, but suddenly found themselves members of a group more restrictive than the authority they had rejected. These cults were usually originated by and centered around a human leader whose needs and desires took priority over those of the members.

THE FAMILY OF LOVE

When a Christian minister named David Berg founded the Children of God in 1968, he said he had a special purpose in life. Since his father was a minister and his mother was an evangelist, it seemed only natural that he would follow in their footsteps. Fed by his own fears and doubts, Berg and his followers became frustrated with society. Among other things Berg predicted that a great earthquake would soon cause California to tumble into the ocean. After moving from California, he and his followers disrupted worship services of Christian congregations in their new home state, Arizona. They became wandering outcasts, often staging protests and demonstrations wherever they went.

David Berg changed his name to "Moses" and encouraged others to change their names to symbolize their "new birth." He withdrew into seclusion and only communicated with his group of followers through his famous "Mo Letters." As Berg's teachings departed further from Scripture, his beliefs and teachings became more radical. He referred to himself as the supreme authority and encouraged his followers to obey him without question.

Berg attacked the authority of the Bible and many Biblical truths, including the virgin birth and the deity of Christ. He encouraged wives to engage in "flirty fishing," recruiting men outside the group using prostitution as bait. Berg claimed that God now approved of this previously forbidden activity.

This group still wanders as nomads in small "family" groups. They are not nearly as significant as they were at the beginning of the explosion of interest in cults in the 1960s.

Objections to groups like the Children of God (Family of Love) center around the authority of the leader and the questionable moral activities encouraged by the leader. Jesus encourages us to test all spirits which come to us **(1 John 4:1).** Scripture also warns that if someone claims to be an angel from heaven but says something which contradicts Scripture, that we are to know that the messenger and the message are not from God **(Gal. 1:8).**

THE MOONIES

The Holy Spirit Association for the Unification of World Christianity, popularly called "The Moonies," was founded by a for-

mer member of the Presbyterian church, Syn Myung Moon. Moon claimed that in 1936 on a hillside in his native Korea he had a vision of Christ. God revealed in the vision that Christ had failed in His earthly mission and that Moon was the one who would complete it.

After success in Korea, Moon brought his church to the United States in 1971 and began recruiting members. His organization reached national prominence when news reports questioned his recruiting techniques. Charges of brainwashing and coercion were leveled against the cult.

Brainwashing and coercion were not the only problems some people had with Moon's religion. Thousands of dollars were raised through the selling of flowers, candy, and other small items. What happened to the money? Cult members promised that the proceeds from the sales would go to help Christian children. Suspicion grew as Moon's personal wealth and prosperity grew. While Moon lived in wealth, most of his church members lived out of vans and on garage floors in poverty. Although most members had never seen Moon, they were willing to sacrifice everything for him and his questionable cause.

Many members who would later talk about the cult had to be kidnapped and deprogrammed in order to be led out of Moon's church. They charged that when they were recruited they had been misled and deceived. Many felt foolish and embarrassed since they had given up everything to someone who was a fraud.

The *Divine Principle* contains the teaching of Moon. This book includes his teachings concerning personal and physical redemption. Although Christ redeemed the world spiritually, Moon declared He died before he married and had children, and therefore failed to redeem the world physically. Moon said that as "perfect parents," he and his third wife would create perfect children and begin populating the earth with a perfect family.

Scripture teaches that anything that detracts from Christ's suffering and death on the cross is not from God. Faith in Jesus' sacrificial death on the cross is the only way to receive forgiveness of sins and eternal life. Many people have been attracted to Moon's teachings because of the recruiting techniques of his "warriors."

THE WAY INTERNATIONAL

The Way International encourages people to join a Bible study. Only later do members of the Bible study group discover that they are not studying the Bible, but instead the beliefs of the group's founder, Victor Paul Wierwille. Wierwille left the Evangelical and Reformed Church when he disagreed with its doctrine.

New recruits must complete a series of 13 three-hour "Power for Abundant Living" classes. While this procedure may seem similar to those followed in other religions, the similarities stop there. Enrollees are required to pay a fee before they can attend classes. No questions are allowed nor may anyone take notes until they have completed the entire course of study. When the course is completed many students experience such a high level of confusion that they can't recall specific questions. Subsequent classes are more detailed and expensive. When new recruits are unable to pay for the classes, they are urged to borrow from their personal friends and relatives.

Wierwille's followers aggressively evangelize by going door-to-door and by forming Bible study groups. Most major Biblical doctrines are denied as members teach that forgiveness and eternal life can be earned only through good works and right living.

The Way International is clearly a group organized around the whims and desires of a human being. Christians who are accustomed to studying the Bible should beware of this attractive, "new" gospel, which is not from God.

SCIENTOLOGY

Scientology is best known through the name of the popular book, *Dianetics*, written by the group's founder, L. Ron Hubbard. This cult began in the 1960s as Hubbard encouraged people to read his book. Hubbard suggested that all human problems, both physical and mental, result from a mental imbalance. This imbalance can be corrected through a process called "auditing."

Scientologists promise to raise an individual's intelligence (IQ) and eliminate all physical and emotional problems simply by having them answer a series of questions while attached to a special meter. When the person's audit on the meter becomes "clear," all problems will cease.

Hubbard began his career as a

science-fiction writer. His claims to have earned advanced engineering degrees and other technical credentials cannot be proved. Like many cult leaders, he withdrew from the public eye and controlled the groups by communicating from seclusion until his recent death.

While Scientology lacks the outward appearance of most religions, it does attract those who seek a peace unsatisfied elsewhere. The sacrificial death of Jesus Christ is regarded as unimportant. Hubbard and his writings replace God's Word as the authority in his church.

HARE KRISHNA

Unlike most of the other cults in this lesson, the International Society for Krishna Consciousness splintered from a non-Christian religion. Founded by His Divine Grace, A. C. Bhaktivedanto Swami Prabhupada, this group gained notoriety in the United States when its founder emigrated from India to the United States. This cult's major goal is reaching "spiritual enlightenment" through "Krishna consciousness." The followers (devotees) spend the bulk of their time chanting and meditating.

Many American travelers have encountered these saffron-robed, chanting cultists in airports and train stations, where they solicit money through the sale of flowers, books, and trinkets. These sales were the main source of income for Krishna followers until wary travelers began steering clear of their robes. Recently, Krishna devotees exchanged their robes for a more typical western style of dress.

This group attracts young people who are having difficulty making life decisions. The rigid and often harsh lifestyle of the Krishna followers offers both security and peace. Krishna devotees drop out of the busy western world and no longer need to make decisions for themselves. All decisions are made for them.

The Hare Krishnas offer a mixture of eastern Hinduism and western Christianity, hoping to attract Christians. This blend of "mind games" and works-righteousness is unacceptable to Biblical Christians who have discovered that only through faith in Jesus Christ is true peace found.

The peace offered by the Krishnas is sticky like flypaper. Once caught, unsuspecting converts have a difficult time gaining their freedom. Christians who trust in the sacrifice of Jesus on the cross find peace in His promise of forgiveness and abundant life, now and in eternity.

THE BAITED AND BARBED HOOK!

Lured and trapped unaware, many people join cults with their eyes wide open. Attracted by the bait, they fail to see the barb on the end of the cult's fishing hook. The barb hooks them securely and prevents escape.

Today, people are in love with and look for a "quick fix" to their problems. Wonder drugs offer instant relief. Computers and calculators complete work with increased efficiency. Labor-saving devices minimize the time spent doing housework and other repetitive tasks. We assume there must be a quick way to fix almost anything. Cult leaders take advantage of this common human desire.

Freedom from God's perfect law is deadly. The laws of cults are based on the whims and desires of a human leader. The forgiveness of sins purchased by Christ's blood becomes unnecessary because many cults teach that sin no longer exists or never did exist.

JESUS NEVER CHANGES

All humans are sinners, and because of their sinful nature rebel against God. We desperately need the love and forgiveness which only the one true God offers through faith in His Son. Thank God that Jesus never changes. Read **Heb. 13:8** and **John 14:6**. What do these passages tell us about Jesus? He suffered, died, and rose so that we could have eternal life. What does God's love for us in Christ Jesus motivate us to do **(Matt. 4:10)**?

TO REVIEW AND REMEMBER

Continue study of the three articles of the Apostles' Creed.

FAMILY TIME

1. Discuss cults which you or members of your family have encountered in the news, at school, at work, at the airport, in a bookstore, etc. Discuss the dangers of cults and how they can be avoided. Agree to pray regularly for one another and for those people who have been caught in the snare of a cult. Ask God to keep you faithful to His Word, as He provides you with the faith-strengthening power to keep your eyes fixed on the cross on which His only Son purchased your forgiveness of sins and eternal life.

2. Study the religion page in the local daily newspaper or the yellow pages in the telephone directory for evidence of cult activity in your area. Discuss ways you and your family can react to cult activity as Christian witnesses in your community. Be prepared to report on your findings at the beginning of the next session.

3. Check out several books on cults from your school, church, or public library. Review the table of contents together. Each family member should become an "expert" on one group. Before the next session have each family member on the "research team" share his/her findings.

Satanic Cults

DISCOVERY POINT

When Jesus conquered sin, death, and the power of the devil, God demonstrated His supreme authority and power over Satan, the counterfeiter, who copies God and tries to lead God's people away from the truth.

MEANING FOR LIFE

People are searching constantly for meaning in life. You may ask some of the questions asked by the individuals in the picture. How would you answer each of the questions? Read **Psalm 139**. How does this psalm answer the questions?

God knew you before you were born and continues to nurture you throughout your life through His Word and Sacraments. The same Spirit of God hovering over the waters at creation **(Genesis 1:2)** is still at work in your life today.

A WAY THAT SEEMS RIGHT

Out of the shadows slithered the enemy, Satan. Disguised as a serpent, God's enemy, the devil, continued what has proven to be the longest and most brutal struggle ever. Scripture doesn't go into great detail about the devil's origin, but it tells us that Satan exists and that he "prowls like a hungry lion."

Further, God's Word helps us to identify his crafty and cunning schemes which attempt to lure us away from the faith God provides for us in Christ Jesus. The names God calls Satan provide us with clues of his masterful deceit. Read each of the following passages and write the name God calls Satan on the blank line beneath the reference.

2 Cor. 11:14

_____

John 8:44

_____

(Means deceiver or liar)

Matt. 12:27

_____

(Means adversary or opponent)

Read **Rev. 12:7–9**. What does this passage describe? Whose final banishment is described in **Rev. 20:7–10**?

"There is a way that seems right to a man, but in the end it leads to death" **(Prov. 14:12)**. In their spiritual search, people often think they have found a "right way." The devil has prepared many counterfeit ways to peace and salvation. Although a way may seem right, unless Christ crucified is at the center, it will always end in death.

SATAN TRICKS ADAM AND EVE

1. God's Word describes Satan's tricks in detail. Satan's strategy is clear from the very first time he attacked people. To the woman he said, "Did God really say, 'You must not eat from any tree in the garden?'" **(Gen. 3:1)**. Satan wanted Adam and Eve to *doubt* God's very words to them. Satan also wants us to *doubt* God's Word and the promises contained in it. How does Satan cause us to *doubt*?

2. After Eve answered the first question, Satan replied, "You will not surely die" **(Gen. 3:4)**. Satan *contradicts* what God said. Satan doesn't want us to listen to God, and so he *contradicts* Him. How does Satan try to *contradict* God in our lives?

3. Satan's third trick is fascinating. "For God knows that when you eat of it your eyes will be opened, and you will be like God, knowing good and evil" **(Gen. 3:5)**. Satan is not content when he causes people to *doubt* God's Word or when he *contradicts* it. Satan *makes promises* of his own: "You will be like God." Although the promise is very attractive, Satan can't keep it. What kinds of promises does Satan make to us?

Satan is tricky. He wants to

destroy us as he attempts to destroy our relationship with God. When we study Satan's attack on Adam and Eve, we can be aware of the strategies he may use to attack us.

SATAN ATTACKS JESUS

Satan was not content to attack God's people—he attacked God Himself. While Jesus was in the wilderness fasting, Satan attacked. Read **Matt. 4:1–11**. Note the schemes Satan used to tempt Jesus. He may use the same tricks on you!

1. "Tell these stones to become bread" **(Matt. 4:3)** may seem like a rather unusual or uncommon temptation. But for a hungry man like Jesus, who had not eaten for 40 days and nights, the temptation was great. Jesus came into the world to serve others by saving them from their sins. Satan tempts Jesus to use His supernatural powers to serve Himself. Satan likewise suggests that we should serve ourselves and not worry about God or others.

2. Satan's second temptation came from the highest point of the temple. Satan said, "Throw yourself down" **(Matt. 4:6)**. In order to add authority to his command to Jesus, Satan quoted a portion of **Psalm 91:** "He will command His angels concerning you, . . . and they will lift you up in their hands, so that you will not strike your foot against a stone."

Satan knew that if Jesus gave into this temptation, it would abruptly halt God's promise of our salvation, the reason for which Jesus came to earth. Satan tempts us to abandon the purposes for which God called us into this world. This sounds pretty clever, but don't forget: Satan's goal for our life is eternal death.

3. In a final attempt to ruin God's plan to save humanity, Satan suggests that in exchange for all the kingdoms of the world Jesus should bow down and worship him **(Matt. 4:9)**. Since the world belongs to God, it wasn't Satan's to offer.

The Old Testament man of God, Isaiah, prophesied that when Jesus came He would be despised, rejected, and suffer **(Is. 53:3)**. Satan tempted Jesus to win the world without suffering. Similarly, when Satan tempts us to take the easy way, we must remember that we too may have to suffer **(Acts 14:22)**. What does **Rom. 8:17** say about suffering in the life of a Christian?

4. Satan approached Jesus with the words, "If you are the Son of God" **(Matt. 4:3, 6)**. Satan also tries to convince us that we are no longer God's children. Satan lies to us, telling us we are ineligible to receive God's forgiveness through Christ, or that we must earn God's acceptance through our own goodness. But these are only lies aimed at robbing us of our saving faith.

By His example, Jesus shows us how to resist Satan's attacks. Each time, Jesus responded to the devil with the words of Holy Scripture. The Bible is the "helmet of salvation" and the "sword of the Spirit" mentioned by Paul in **Eph. 6:17**. Paul describes many pieces of armor provided by God for our defense and protection. Our offensive weapon is God's Word. Use it, and Satan will flee from you. In the third verse of Martin Luther's famous hymn, "A Mighty Fortress Is Our God" (LW 298), we are told that "one little word can fell him!" That one little word is *Jesus*.

Jesus defeated Satan when He suffered and died on the cross. He proclaimed His victory over the power of Satan on Easter morning when He rose victorious from the grave.

Satan still actively tempts people in the world today, but Christ is stronger. "No, in all these things we are more than conquerors through Him who loved us" **(Rom. 8:37)**.

SAY YOU LOVE SATAN

> NORTHPORT, LONG ISLAND—Police arrested Ricky Kasso, 17, and James Troiano, 18, on charges of second-degree murder. Both were members of a satanic group called "Knights of the Black Circle," which had been spray-painting satanic symbols in a local park for several years.
>
> Sometime during the night of June 16, 1984, members of this group led 17-year-old Gary Lauwers into the woods and conducted a four-hour ritual in which they burned Lauwer's clothing and hair, and then stabbed him to death. Lauwers shouted during the attack, "I love you, Mom." At the same time Ricky Kasso commanded, "No! Say you love Satan."
>
> Two days after his arrest, Ricky Kasso hanged himself in his jail cell. Jimmy Troiano was later acquitted on all charges. Concerned teens from the area spent time during the investigation and trial cleaning up the vandalism and graffiti caused by the gang. ("Drugs and the Devil on Long Island," *Newsweek*, July 23, 1984.)

SATAN TRIES TO ECLIPSE GOD

Incredible as it may seem, some people worship the devil. Evidence suggests that interest in the occult and devil worship is on the rise.

The great counterfeiter, Satan, is interested in gaining followers. He will use any means possible to bring people into his clutches. Wherever God builds a church, Satan builds a chapel. He will lie, cheat, and steal, masquerading as an angel of light **(2 Cor. 11:14)** and, if necessary, as God.

Read the following passages and describe what Scripture warns us concerning the devil and his influence before the second coming of Christ.

1 Tim. 4:1

_____

_____

2 Tim. 3:1

_____

_____

Matt. 24:10–12

_____

_____

There are three major types of Satanists which we will examine—religious Satanists, satanic cults, and self-styled Satanists.

RELIGIOUS SATANISTS

Modern Satanism can be traced back to Aleister Crowley who was born in England in 1875. He rebelled against his strict Christian upbringing, yet sought supernatural guidance. Although Crowley couldn't actually be called a Satanist, the things he wrote about were satanic. Crowley took great delight in shocking his parents, friends, and especially his very religious uncle with completely repulsive and unreligious acts. He made a pact with the devil, wrote poems honoring murders, publicly called the Queen of England dirty names, engaged in homosexual activity, and encouraged the free use of sex and drugs.

For Crowley, the United States was the perfect place to try out his ideas since the United States allowed religious freedom. Crowley advocated complete freedom to do anything. He believed that Satan was more powerful than God, and he ridiculed Christ as impotent. Descriptions of his drug experiences suggest that he died in a cheap boarding house after injecting himself daily with 11 grams of pure heroine. When he died in 1947, he left the seeds of modern Satanism which would be planted by Anton LaVey.

THE FIRST CHURCH OF SATAN

In 1966 a former circus performer named Anton Szandor LaVey proclaimed that God was dead and the age of Satan had begun. "Satan lives" became a password to the rituals conducted at the headquarters of his church in San Francisco. Many Christians believe his group to be quite dangerous, but possibly less harmful than other groups which operate underground.

LaVey's highly popular book, which encouraged Satanism, was *The Satanic Bible*. It outsells the Holy Bible on many college campuses. Some read it out of curiosity. It is often found at crime scenes along with other clues of satanic rituals. If followed, LaVey's teachings pose a serious threat to Christians.

The cornerstone of LaVey's beliefs are his "Nine Satanic Statements" from *The Satanic Bible*. These statements detail his philosophy which attracts people from every walk of life.

1. Satan represents indulgence, instead of abstinence.
2. Satan represents vital existence, instead of spiritual pipe dreams.
3. Satan represents undefiled wisdom, instead of hypocritical self-deceit.
4. Satan represents kindness to those who deserve it, instead of love wasted on ingrates.
5. Satan represents vengeance, instead of turning the other cheek.
6. Satan represents responsibility to the responsible, instead of concern for psychic vampires.
7. Satan represents man as just another animal, sometimes better, more often worse than those that walk on all fours, who because of his "divine spiritual and intellectual development" has become the most vicious animal of all.
8. Satan represents all of the so-called sins, as they all lead to physical, mental, or emotional gratification.
9. Satan has been the best friend the church has ever had, since he has kept it in business all these years.

Other organized satanic groups include the Temple of Set, the Process Church of the Final Judgment, and the Worldwide Church of Satanic Liberation. There are at least 450 other identifiable satanic groups in the United States alone. Many are secret and don't publish any information about themselves. Occasionally, evidence of their existence surfaces.

SATANIC CULTS

A satanic cult is a group which has splintered from one of the visible groups mentioned in the last section. They are called cults because their behavior deviates from and is usually more radical than their parent group. Aleister Crowley was affiliated with many different Satanic/magic groups. Some of the practices of these groups remain in many satanic cults today. The Process Church of the Final Judgment broke away from LaVey's Satanic Church and later went underground.

Satanic activities are often reported in the newspapers. Most police departments can't afford the time to investigate every allegation of satanic worship. According to current laws, the harmless rituals conducted by many of these groups are not illegal. But when their ceremonies expand to include animal sacrifice, burglary, arson, grave desecration, and human sacrifice, police investigation and legal action are necessary.

SELF-STYLED SATANISTS

Unlike the other two categories, the so-called self-styled Satanists lack organization and structure. Their behavior is more bizzare than either of the other two groups. As a result these self-styled groups are considered the most dangerous. Ordinary citizens are most likely to come into contact with and join a self-styled satanic group.

Since self-styled groups operate independently, several groups may perform identical rituals without being aware that other groups exist. They all have similar beliefs about Satan and seek to harness the powers of evil and wickedness. They are all tied together with a common thread—worship of and allegiance to Satan. Incidents such as the one reported in *Newsweek* occur frequently, indicating a rapid increase of Satanism.

Since most of the news reports relate teenage involvement in activities of self-styled Satanists, we may think that all self-styled Satanists are young. While many Satanists become interested and involved at an early age, there are also many older self-styled Satanists.

Self-styled Satanists follow patterns set by Crowley, but also belong to and share ideas from several different groups. The rituals of most self-styled Satanists include some type of sacrifice. Reports of animal sacrifices are met with cries of disgust. Reports of human sacrifice are increasing with frightening incidence!

Most self-styled Satanists begin their involvement with innocent contact, perhaps through a friend, at a party, or a night club. Drugs and sexual activities are usually a significant part of their involvement. Self-styled satanic groups conduct rituals that trace their roots back to the "Black Mass" of the Middle Ages.

In a May 16, 1985 segment entitled "Devil Worshipers" on the ABC News program, "20/20," reporter Tom Jarrel suggested that self-styled Satanists learn about Satanism from three major sources: books, music, and movies. Standing in a shopping mall of an affluent New York City suburb, Jarrel pointed out three stores, side by side, each offering information about the occult—a bookstore, a music store, and a video rental store.

Fantasy games such as *Dungeons and Dragons* include pretend occult magic, casting spells, and involvement in a spirit world. These games play a significant role in introducing unsuspecting young people to the powers of occult magic and Satanism.

WHAT TO DO ABOUT SATANISM?

"[Name], do you renounce the devil and all his works and all his ways?" When have you heard this question before? At our baptism we renounced Satan. (We also answer this question when we are confirmed.) We must daily renounce Satan as we recall God's choosing us to be His children through Holy Baptism. Martin Luther suggested that upon rising each day, Christians should make the sign of the cross and remember what God did for them in Holy Baptism. Ask yourself, "Have I opened any doors which might allow Satan to enter even a tiny corner of my life? Are there lingering doubts in my mind through which Satan could confuse me?"

As Christians, we have the privilege of turning to God for forgiveness of all the evil we have thought or done. In Christ we have forgiveness for all sins, including those "hidden faults" which have crept in unawares or which we have forgotten **(Ps. 19:12)**.

In our thoughts, speech, and actions, we can rely upon God and the power of the Holy Spirit to close the door on Satan so he cannot enter our lives. God in Christ has already won the victory over Satan and all other forces of evil. Because of Jesus we can face all evil with the confident assurance that the One within us is greater than the one who is in the world **(1 John 4:4)**.

TO REVIEW AND REMEMBER

Conclude the review of the Apostles' Creed and memorize one of the following Bible passages:

■ "Therefore put on the full armor of God, so that when the day of evil comes, you may be able to stand your ground . . ." **(Eph. 6:13)**.

■ "Submit yourselves, then, to God. Resist the devil, and he will flee from you" **(James 4:7)**.

FAMILY TIME

1. Discuss with your family evidences of Satanism. Which movies, books, and magazine articles include references to the occult or Satanism? Which music refers to the devil or satanic rituals? Where have you heard about Satanism in the news?

2. Read **Eph. 6:10–18** and discuss each piece of armor provided by God. Discuss the importance of each piece. Talk about how you wield the "sword of the Spirit." Remember to pray for each other at all times.

3. Are you aware of the fact that Satan wishes to devour you **(1 Peter 5:8–9)**? Satan is not content to trouble or confuse you. He wants to totally destroy you. Read **Matt. 4:1–11**. Praise God for His victory over Satan.

22–2345
0–570–09752–5